"This book convinces me that this sister and I have much in common. I can learn a lot from her. In fact, I have learned a lot from her. I benefit from her hard-earned wisdom. I am inspired by an eloquence that grew from her own healing. And you too are in for an experience of healing, learning, and inspiration."

—FROM THE FOREWORD BY ARTHUR BOERS

"This book is so rich, and I find myself whirling with the fullness of it. I want to spend time working with it—reflecting, chewing, digesting, being challenged and nourished, and held by it—slowly. For me, each chapter has been an invitation to seek, to listen deep inside, and to find the ways in which God reaches out to me."

—DAWN ZAK, RETREAT FACILITATOR, MILWAUKEE, WI

"An excellent facilitation guide on growth and healing for small group retreats, book discussions, or self-guided reflection and contemplation."

—BRIAN STAHLKOPF, LICENSED PROFESSIONAL COUNSELOR, MILWAUKEE, WI

THIS MOMENT OF RETREAT

THIS MOMENT OF RETREAT

Listening to the Birch, the Milkweed, and
the Healing Song in All that is Now

HEATHER LEE

FOREWORD BY
ARTHUR BOERS

RESOURCE *Publications* · Eugene, Oregon

I dedicate this book to
my family:
Wes, Mollee, and Andy,

my friends:
by God's grace, too many to name,

and to my God:
*in faith that I am doing Your will by sharing
my writing, my music, and my experience.*

CONTENTS

CHAPTER 1

THE BIRCH TREE

*For moments of
waiting and growth*

1

CHAPTER 2

GATHER THE FRAGMENTS

*For moments of hunger
and abundance*

9

CHAPTER 3

HARVEST

*For moments of emptying
and fruitfulness*

15

HOW TO ACCESS
SONG FILES

Readers can access the songs in the following ways.

1. **Author's website or Facebook page**
   free mp3 files and links to YouTube
   follow these links:

   http://www.heatherleeonline.com

   https://www.facebook.com/heatherleeonline

2. **Purchase on iTunes**
   at the following links:

   https://itunes.apple.com/us/album/she-stands/
   id413774802?uo=4

   https://itunes.apple.com/us/album/into-the-light/
   id509383758?uo=4

3. **Purchase on cd baby**
   at the following links:

   http://www.cdbaby.com/cd/heatherlee

   http://www.cdbaby.com/cd/heatherlee2

FOREWORD

By Arthur Boers

Full disclosure: Heather Lee is a friend twice removed. My good friend Daniel introduced me to his good friend David, who in turn told Heather about me and me about Heather. (All this without the benefits of Facebook.) While I was more than happy to read the manuscript—and listen to the songs and music—of a friend of a friend's friend, I had no idea what to expect. I did it on faith and was richly rewarded.

I quickly discovered a kindred spirit. Heather Lee has an eloquent way with words, shown both in the prose and the poetic songs in this book, not to mention the epiphanies she experiences along the way. And her music is heartening, hopeful, and healing.

Soon, my reading of Heather's manuscript was not an assignment or a commitment. Rather, it became a way for me to enter into prayer, to reflect on my own life, and to connect with God.

I admire Heather's sense of self-deprecating humor. As someone who is an off-the-scale Myers-Briggs "J," I love her line about being a "recovering planner." Her poems speak deeply to my own condition and yearnings. And her countercultural take on what it means to thrive and grow is one that I cannot hear too often.

In fact, many phrases here that brought me up short and invited me to ponder, "the discipline of the shift," "grounded gently," "the washing of our souls in song," "the largeness of each moment."

As a hiker, an aspiring pray-er, a music appreciator, I was heartened by this book. I trust that you will be too.

Heather and I have never met. We live in different countries. She has talents that I can only envy from afar. And yet this book convinces me that this sister and I have much in common. I can learn a lot from her. In fact, I have learned a lot from her. I benefit from her hard-earned wisdom. I am inspired by an eloquence that grew from her own healing. And you too are in for an experience of healing, learning, and inspiration as you explore the following pages.

As we have never met face-to-face, I would likely not recognize Heather if we happened to bump into each other on the street. Yet her distinct voice is one that I suspect I would recognize anywhere. I hope we hear a lot more from her.

Arthur Boers

Author of *Living into Focus:*
Choosing What Matters in an Age of Distractions

and

The Way is Made by Walking:
A Pilgrimage Along the Camino de Santiago.

PREFACE

There isn't a cloud in the sky on an early summer afternoon as I sit with my journal and my dog in the backyard. I am a few short days away from submitting my first book, *This Moment of Retreat*, to the publisher after the fall, winter, and spring learning process of editing, revising, doubting, sharing, and celebrating that has brought me here to this cloudless summer day. It must be time.

With what shall I preface the book? I realize that I write very little about summertime and cloudless moments. The retreat chapters ahead were written mostly in other seasons. As I shake my head and smile at myself, I guess I don't need to wonder why. Summer is my Sabbath time without even needing to attend to it as such. And, the seasons are always turning, aren't they? Summer succumbs to the harvest and death of the colorful fall that lets go to the cold waiting of winter, which melts into the struggle and new growth of the spring seed, which delights, blossoms, and rests in the return, again, to the warmth and light of summertime. I exist from and in a deeper place in the summer, and God's healing touch just seems more accessible—like it hangs in the humid, teeming air that engulfs me and all of creation. Knowing this summer place in myself provides guidance. I can recognize it as the place that I am often reaching for and trying to touch in other seasons of my life. It all comes around, again, and again, and again, but summer is a great place to start.

Not unlike many Midwesterners, my family has a place on a lake *up north* (an expression that refers to a getaway place anywhere north of where we are). It is my summer place. It holds depth, stillness, warmth, light, and an ancient and eternal connection for me. On the 4th of July holiday, my extended family gathers there, and, it seems, we all find a place to rest in ourselves, in God, in beauty, and in the many ways that *summer at the lake* gives in abundance to each of us. We have few cares except to sit and watch the loons raise their babies and to listen to them cry out over the water in search of each other. In that summer loon cry, though, beneath cloudless summer skies, there is a haunting call—a song that reminds of longing, of deeper love, of loss, of babies growing up, of summers gone, of a deeper summer ahead, of a need to listen, heal, and grow, and to receive the next season to do it. I invite you, as a preface, to listen to and sing a summer song as you start this journey with me and to hear that call that will take you into this moment of retreat.

THE HEALING SONG OF NOW
THE LOONS

Not a cloud in the sky.
Fourth of July.
Lake's buzzin' shallow and deep.
The loons float on by.
I've not a care in the world except for the loons.

Calling, ooooooooooooooh
Calling, ooooooooooooooh
Calling, ooooooooooooooh
Calling, baby, sweet baby, where are you?

Grandma's frying the eggs.
Mom is shining the bar.
Sister's singing old hymns
as she strums her guitar.
I've not a care in the world except for the loons.

Calling, oooooooooooooh
Calling, oooooooooooooh
Calling, oooooooooooooh
Calling, baby, sweet baby, where are you?

Kids are soaked to the bones.
They've got fire on their minds.
Flames of sunshine and rockets
shine in their eyes.
I've not a care in the world except for the loons.

Grandpa's revving his boat.
Uncle's pounding a nail.
Dad's grilling his catch.
The dog's chasing her tail.
My heart's free as a bird,
maybe free as the loon.
How she haunts me with a song that says
that free hearts call out too . . . ooooooooooh.

Calling, oooooooooooooh
Calling, oooooooooooooh
Calling, oooooooooooooh
Calling, baby, sweet baby, where are you?

ACKNOWLEDGMENTS

I wish to express my gratitude for this non-exhaustive list of people who have provided guidance, love, encouragement, help, humble service, and generosity to me in the writing of this book. I acknowledge:

My *girlfriends*, my spiritual sisters, bearing witness to the growth from this journey and helping to edit it too:

Amy, Colleen, Lisa, Marita, Dawn, Ellen, Tracy, Cindy, Lindsey, and Kim

The authors who graciously offered time and contribution to this, my first book:

Arthur Boers who wrote the Foreword

Pastor Fred Reklau who proofread and copy-edited the manuscript

INTRODUCTION

This moment sings the soul of an angel
will you tend to its rhyme?
Its melody fills you,
silences keep you
in blooms hidden under the vine.
On fleeting blue wings,
the butterfly sings
to the blind stampede going by.
The song becomes cries
as this moment dies.
And Now a new moment arrives.

The soul of this moment asks, "Do you have a moment? Do you have a moment to tend to my song?" Can you hear it? Slow down. Listen. Quiet. Still. Breathe. Do you hear the song of this moment—its melodies and sweet silences? Do you notice the fragile blooms underneath the vines of your busy days? Do you hear the guidance of angels that point you to the beauty of the butterfly? Could this moment be a moment of retreat? Will you step away, courageously, from the blind stampede and attend to, listen to, and delight in this moment of retreat?

Welcome, my friend, to this new moment. This is a moment of retreat—a moment of retreat to the present—a moment to listen, see, and breathe—a moment free of distraction from yesterday and tomorrow—free from the time on the clock. This is a moment of retreat—of retreat to the song of the here and now sung by the birch, the milkweed, and all of creation. Yes, *all of creation* is singing in every moment, and, if attended to, can provide melodies, words, rhythms, and silences that heal brokenness, encourage growth, and deepen relationship with God for all who listen.

These moments of retreat are eternally available. They can be one deep breath or even one shallow breath. They can be thirty minutes of meditation at the beginning of a day or an outdoor walk in city or woods. These moments can be a weekend of solitude at a retreat center, a day of solitude at home, or even the prayerful attention to a five-minute song. There can be—in fact there *is*—retreat available in this very moment. Moments of retreat beg more moments of retreat, and, over time, can teach a way of *being* in each moment. They teach life as ceaseless prayer and a call to deeper engagement with *God in all*—in each moment that is given—to heal and to grow.

Being in each moment is not what society, church, school, or family taught me. I learned *doing*—working, caretaking, fixing, worrying, producing, competing, judging, planning, controlling, holding on—doing, doing, doing. Moments of retreat have challenged me with teachings of *being*—stillness, openness, unhurriedness, non-judgment, powerlessness, creativity, acceptance, letting go—being, being, being. Unlearning the old takes many moments of retreat, but the moments are always there. Actually, they are not *there*, but *here*—now. I simply must be disciplined in my attention to them. This book is a humble companion to developing a discipline of retreat, something to grant you encouragement, permission, guidance, and connection in your own moments of retreat.

I am called by the great Creator, that divine Holy Spirit that moves us all, to write during my own journey of unlearning, of healing, and of growth. I am a middle-aged woman: wife of eighteen years and counting, mother of two children, daughter, sister, friend, advanced-degreed, full-time accounting and business instructor (yes, really), board member, volunteer, church lay leader—on and on—but these descriptions are not who I am. I simply . . . am. I am a human being—living, breathing, learning, discovering, encouraging, healing, praying, singing—a human being, a child of God, just like you. I am new to this moment, just like you. I am. I am. I am.

I am always in need of healing and help. I am a recovering planner, controller, caretaker, enabler, fixer, people-pleasing perfectionist. Many of these tendencies are attributed to codependent people, those who live or have lived with some form of addiction in their lives. Yes, that is true, and I also venture to say that we live in an addicted, or at least deeply distracted, society. This society is what forms us. There are few, if any, untouched by addiction— a disease of needing something, using something, searching for something outside of oneself—and more and more of it (alcohol, drugs, food, sex, social media, shopping, television, gambling, approval, attention, validation, to be needed, power, prestige, glory, and on and on) to provide what can only come from God within, the great *I Am*, eternally available in this and each moment. ". . . I am who I am . . ." (Exodus 3:14) We need healing, and we need help. We need guidance to change the patterns that fuel the brokenness in our addicted and distracted lives. God is in this moment with that help.

God's help and healing have come to me through what I now name as moments of retreat. Much of my deeper, creative exploration and healing came in moments of multi-day, silent, personal retreat, but the moments of retreat started much more simply as a daily morning discipline of quiet time with words of Scripture. Inviting the Word into the moment has always provided me an anchor, or perhaps a rudder or an oar, that gently guides and holds the conversation with the rest of the flow of creation in that moment. I have also been guided through the words of other devotional authors like Joyce Rupp, Henri Nouwen, Mark Nepo, Thomas Merton, John Main, Julia Cameron, Wayne Muller, Arthur Boers, Theresa of Avila, and many others, unnamed here or anonymous. The authors we are reading in the moment are part of that moment. I am grateful to be part of yours. As my connection to God grew through this discipline of quiet time with words, the moment got bigger, and I became more attentive and aware of God reaching out to lead me—in prayer and meditation; in nature; in journaling; in music; in other people; and in myself. The moments became spacious and filled with healing song.

In listening to the richness of each moment, I have been guided through a gateway to a life filled with moments of sacredness and retreat. "Very truly I tell you, I am the gate . . . ," says Jesus (John 10:7). Each moment, I can step through the gate into the vastness of God's creation, guidance, and beauty. These moments have called me to respond and to grow. I have learned and practice daily, silent meditation. I participate in my spiritual communities in different ways than I had previously in ministries like healing, prayer, song, and spiritual growth. I am faithful to daily listening walks in God's great creation (often, this includes my dog), to a yoga practice, to creative writing, and to semi-annual, silent, multi-day personal retreats. At these silent retreats, primarily at monasteries, I am reminded, each time I return, that I have more to learn. In that humility, I ask God to teach me, again, how to open myself to the moment and be led. I listen to the stillness inside—to God's call in those moments. Though it has seldom been an easy path, I have been deeply guided and healed. I have been called, sometimes quite strongly, to respond, as co-creator—in writing, yes, and ultimately, in the words, melodies, and voice of song.

The Birch, The Milkweed, and the songs of the chapters that follow are songs born out of my moments of retreat that I voiced to creation and to God as I healed. These songs became an antiphonal response—a sort of back and forth similar to the verses of the Psalms—to the healing song being sung to me—by the butterflies, the blooms, and the angels in the moment. "I am going to send an angel in front of you, to guard you on the way and to bring you to the place that I have prepared. Be attentive to him and listen to his voice . . ." (Exodus 23:20-21). *This moment sings the soul of an angel* and I respond, as I am led, by joining the song.

ORGANIZATION OF
THIS MOMENT OF RETREAT

I have organized this companion book of retreat into seven chapters centered in seven songs of healing. In the Christian tradition, the seventh day is the Sabbath day. I encourage you to consider and claim a moment of retreat as Sabbath—holy—be it every seventh day, seventh week, seventh hour, seventh minute, seventh second, every seventh breath. I imagine you, dear reader, are considering the discipline of the shift. You could begin now. You need only take a small step and ask God to help.

The retreat topics are centered on healing. Implicit in this is the claim that we come to the moment burdened with some brokenness or darkness. I have found in my own retreat time that claiming or confessing that darkness, as honestly as I am able, and bringing it humbly and vulnerably to God in the moment facilitates healing and creates beauty in the process. The themes of each chapter are provided with each song title so that you can select one that calls to your particular situation at the moment you are seeking to retreat. The chapters can be read in any order and at any pace, be it one word, one sentence, one section, or an entire chapter at a time. God will lead that process for you.

Scriptural Grounding and Inspiration

Each of the seven chapters is grounded gently in a Scriptural verse. I say gently as I do not wish for this to exclude those who have doubts about church or religion. It is not necessary to embrace all of Christianity or belong to a church or religious organization to claim a relationship with God through the words and teachings in the Bible. If a verse from Scripture is singing in your moment, so be it. Trust it. Listen to it. Sing with it. Allow it in as a guide and conversation partner. I have many deeply spiritual friends, alienated from the church as an institution, who long to give themselves permission to find God in Scripture. If this is you, you have permission, now, in this moment. Go ahead. I also have many deeply spiritual church-going friends who believe that, for some reason, they are not qualified or educated enough to interpret or read Scripture. As I recall, the first disciples were fishermen or other working folks. I am but a lay person, as well. God will find you, right where you are, with Scripture. Go ahead. You have permission.

Experience, Strength, and Hope Reflection Embracing the Moment in All of Creation

In each of the seven chapters, grounded in Scripture and song, there is a devotional reflection on the moments of retreat in which my healing song was initially inspired, which includes images of all of Creation. When you begin to open up to the largeness of each moment, you will find God speaking to you in almost everything. These reflections offer some of the pieces of my moments that spoke to me, guided me, and called out to me. I share them with you in hopes that they mingle in your moment to heal, guide, inspire, and encourage. As mentioned, in a call for healing, there is an owning of brokenness in these reflections. It is often from the deepest darkness that new life springs. That has been true for me. Sharing our experience and strength in moments of darkness requires courage, vulnerability, and faith and can provide deeply needed strength and hope to the world.

Meditation and Prayer

I have included a prayer and meditation suggestion that invites you to apply the theme of each chapter in conversation with God in the moment. Conversation is two-way, listening and responding, receiving and giving. There are ideas in this section to explore both sides—meditation and prayer. Listening walks, silent meditation, poetry reading, prayers, and breath work are all found here.

The Healing Song of Now

Listen and respond. Listen and respond. Listen and respond to the actual song of the retreat. Music and lyrics are provided for each retreat—music and lyrics that I wrote, humbly, imperfectly, often crying out in a force of creative energy from God to God, in the moment. Listen and respond. Listen and sing. Don't be afraid to sing. So often, we judge our voices harshly. Have you ever been caught saying, "I can't sing"? Oh, how we cut ourselves off from the washing of our souls in song. God used both my fear and love of singing to teach me to embrace imperfection, to learn the beauty and necessity of making mistakes, and to love the process of healing and growth. I was not in touch with myself as a singer, songwriter, poet, or writer until I started this journey (remember, I am an accounting professor—safe, safe, safe). You will undoubtedly be surprised by what you are called to and by the fears you must face to respond. Embrace and honor all without judgment. Encourage. Sing.

Questions for the Moment

Finally, the chapters conclude with questions for your moments of retreat that are woven from the earlier Scripture, reflections, prayers, and songs. These questions can be used for journaling and creative writing, but, of course, you must respond to the questions that come to you from your own moments of retreat, of which this little companion guidebook is only one piece. Contained in the journaling questions is also the encouragement to explore what is stirring in you as a response to the moment. Do you have a call to write a poem, paint a picture, do a dance, or sing a new song? Do you feel a nudge to take a walk, sit in silence, talk to a friend, or start some new venture? References to other Scriptural passages that relate to the themes of the particular moment of retreat are also provided.

WAYS TO USE THIS BOOK

God will guide the use of this book in the moments it is found in. Here are several ways to consider its use.

1. Personal Retreat. Find a retreat center and schedule an overnight, weekend, or full week retreat. Select a chapter of the book to guide your time, and let God lead you.

2. Daily Devotional Reading. Establish a daily discipline of prayer and retreat time (now is a good time to start). Spend some time each day in silent meditation, prayer, reading, writing, or singing. Include a word, a sentence, a prayer, a song, or a question from this book in this sacred time.

3. Spiritual Book Group. Invite others in your family, church, or other spiritual community to explore the book together. Read, pray, reflect, discuss, sing, and share the process.

4. Group Retreat. Lead, plan, or attend a group women's retreat, men's retreat, couple's retreat, family retreat, or other community retreat. Select a chapter to organize and guide the group's time and discussions.

5. Bible Study. Use the Scripture passage and following chapter material for a group Bible study.

6. Worship. Incorporate poetry, prayer, and songs from the book into your worship services.

THE CALL TO AND HOPE
FOR HEALING AND PEACE

I share my experience, strength, and hope in this companion retreat guide as a call to, and a means of, loving service: to heal you, me, and the world, and to inspire others to unlearn and to let go of patterns that are preventing them from living in the vastness of this very moment, a moment in which they meet their God, the great Creator, the writer of the great song that we are all a part of, the compassionate, loving, forgiving presence that is within and without and available to all, right where we are. My hope for you is healing and peace. Peace to you in all of your moments of retreat.

Heather Lee

CHAPTER 1

THE BIRCH TREE

*For moments of
waiting and growth*

SCRIPTURAL GROUNDING
AND INSPIRATION

First Corinthians 13: 1–13

If I speak in the tongues of mortals and of angels, but do not have love, I am a noisy gong or a clanging cymbal. And if I have prophetic powers, and understand all mysteries and all knowledge, and if I have all faith, so as to remove mountains, but do not have love, I am nothing. If I give away all my possessions, and if I hand over my body so that I may boast, but do not have love, I gain nothing. Love is patient; love is kind; love is not envious or boastful or arrogant or rude. It does not insist on its own way; it is not irritable or resentful; it does not rejoice in wrongdoing, but rejoices in the truth. It bears all things, believes all things, hopes all things, endures all things. Love never ends. But as for prophecies, they will come to an end; as for tongues, they will cease; as for knowledge, it will come to an end. For we know only in part, and we prophesy only in part; but when the complete comes, the partial will come to an end.

When I was a child, I spoke like a child, I thought like a child, I reasoned like a child; when I became an adult, I put an end to childish ways. For now we see in a mirror, dimly, but then we will see face to face. Now I know only in part; then I will know fully, even as I have been fully known. And now faith, hope, and love abide, these three; and the greatest of these is love.

EXPERIENCE, STRENGTH, AND HOPE
REFLECTION—EMBRACING THE
MOMENT IN ALL OF CREATION

In contemplation of waiting and growth, I set off one beautiful, mid-winter morning, the sun shining, into the woods. It was the second day of a retreat that rested in First Corinthians and the many natures of love and loving. I was struggling deeply with my own new growth, and I was uncertain and frustrated in discerning what God's call to love was asking of me. My prayer was for openness and listening to what my situation had to teach me and for guidance on what action, if any, to take. The lake and the woods beckoned me as the outdoors usually does when I am in a funk. At the edge of the woods just before I reached a field, I was called to stop and engage a birch tree.

This birch tree stood tall, white, and glorious in the snow-covered, sunny morning. It had a very large, beautiful piece of bark pulled away and unwrapping itself from the tree right at my eye level. I inspected it, touched it, tugged it gently, thinking, as I always do, that, perhaps, I could help the tree release it, but it was solidly in place. I left it there. *Let it grow.* Beneath this stubborn, peeling piece of bark was a soft piece of new growth, new skin, new bark, brand new, not toughened by the harsh winters yet. I put my cheek up against it. It was so soft, like my skin, warm from the sun, and tender. It seemed vulnerable, yet beautiful as new growth often is. I rested my cheek there for a while, thinking about the vulnerability of my own new growth—how soft, how tender, and clinging tightly—how I longed for it to be protected, admired, found beautiful. *It is beauty.*

I looked further at the tree and noticed that there were a few pieces of very old bark that had probably unraveled and held on years ago. Some were, finally, dry and blackened, easily brushed off by me or to be blown off by the winds of the future. The tree had held onto those pieces long enough, and now they were easily, and clearly, to be let go. Still, some of the peeled bark from years ago remained firmly attached, likely never to be released. They were to be held as part of the beauty and identity of the tree.

That piece of newly peeled bark that initially caught my eye was not nearly ready to be let go. In fact, it was standing strong and firm, almost protecting the new growth beneath it. Both held such beauty in different ways. The old, strong bark—firm, weathered, colored, somewhat inflexible, separated from the tree but boldly holding on and claiming its spot in the sunlight—said *"hold on to the old, you need it still."* The soft, pure white, new bark—clinging closely and tightly to where it was growing from the tree itself, vulnerable and soft—said *"newness is beauty, let it show."*

I put my arms around the tree (really, I did, tree-hugger at heart), my cheek pressed against that new bark. We were *face to face.* Standing in the sun, I felt God, the Creator, return the embrace. In it, I felt the complexity and the simplicity of love, patient and enduring. The message revealed was, *"Wait. It's all okay, in fact, all beautiful. Let it unfold."* As I walked away, I felt a deep sense of loss, a desire to run back and experience it again, but also a deep sense of peace and knowledge of God's warm, gentle, abiding presence and love for me, and perhaps also a bit of hope, which is what I needed most.

Maybe a full year later, I retreated again to the winter woods. I remained challenged by waiting, but I had let the new growth show. I had written the first song of my life at age thirty-eight after that winter encounter with God and the birch tree. Even with the healing balm of that song and the creative process of voicing it, I had open wounds when it came to some dimensions of love. It so happens I met with another birch tree on this walk too. This tree was less grand than the first, but beautiful. The only thing I remember was that it was split open, perhaps by lightning, but growing healthy toward the sky. It sang hope to me—bear all things, believe all things—hope once again.

MEDITATION AND PRAYER

Find an opportunity to stand face to face with a tree—a birch tree if you can find one, but any tree will do. Consider what this tree has to teach you about growth, about waiting, about the natures of love—in particular, patience and endurance. Notice any wounds the tree wears. If you are so inclined, wrap your arms around the tree and feel its strength. What does is tell you? Stand as tall as you can and place your arms in the air. Feel your feet rooted to the earth, and your arms reaching for the sky, and all of you— wounded and alive—in between. When you are ready to end your time with the tree, read the poem of prayer that follows.

Face to Face with the Wounded Birch
A Poem of Meditation and Prayer

Birch tree is split
from foundation to face.
Skin visibly severed
split open—a space.
A space to peer into,
a space over to cry,
cut deep and too long,
yet the tree didn't die.

There's green at its feet
its arms in the air
grounded and reaching
like the wound isn't there.
Bearing all things
and wearing its pain
rejoicing in sunshine,
and hoping in rain.

What faith shows this tree,
and what love in its grace.
Wisdom is granted
when we see face to face.
I, too, stand severed.
God, place my arms in the air.
Make me grounded and reaching
like the wound isn't there . . . Amen.

THE HEALING SONG OF NOW
BIRCH TREE

Find a quiet place to listen to the song, *Birch Tree*. Read or sing along with the song. Make no judgments about how you are participating in the song. Your voice and the way music moves in you is beautiful and can call you to a place of winter wandering through the woods. Notice which parts of the song call out to you and linger there. Feel the words and the music drawing you to a place that needs healing, growth, or exploration.

Lyrics to *Birch Tree*

Sun shining, snow gleaming
Can You help me out of here
see anything clear?
New growth and old promises
through a lifetime of fear
go slowly, my dear.

Sun shining (speak to me) snow gleaming
(call to me)

Did I know love before?
Do I know it today?
Did I know love before?
Can you show me the way?
That birch tree stands strong.
It beckons to me.
I think God is answering
and wants me to see.

God speak to me, God call
God speak to me, God call (call to me)

I'm wandering lost
in the sun through the snow.
Can it be just as simple
as letting it grow?

Teach me to let it go slow
to see it as beauty as it unfolds.

Sun shining (speak to me) snow gleaming
(call to me)

Teach me, teach me to grow.
Teach me to let the new show
and hold on to the old that's not ready to go.

QUESTIONS FOR THE MOMENT

1. How are you growing at the moment? What is new and vulnerable? What piece of you is starting to peel away but is not nearly ready to be let go of? Consider how you, or someone else, might be trying to tear it away before it is ready? How is that part standing in watch or in guard of the new? What old pieces of you are simply parts of you that will never be let go? What old pieces of yourself have been easily brushed away?

2. Waiting with patience is part of growth and part of love. In what ways is it hard for you to practice waiting? What qualities of love are required of you? How could listening to this moment help you to cultivate these qualities? What do you hear about hope?

3. What wounds do you carry with you? Are you able to wear them with the grace and life of the wounded birch? How have they brought you closer to seeing the perfect love of God? What is fearful about looking at and revealing the wounds? How might God help you grow because of your wounds? Explore the idea that the process of growth is one of beauty.

4. What natures of love do you seem to have an easy time with, and what parts are most difficult for you? How has God's love, which encompasses the easy and the difficult pieces, been an example to you in your life and your relationship with yourself and others?

5. How does the prayer and song of the birch tree help you heal and grow?

6. What is stirring in you as a response to the moment? Do you have a creative call or something stronger to write a poem, paint a picture, do a dance, or sing a new song? Do you feel a nudge to take a walk, sit in silence, talk to a friend, or start some new venture? Try it. What encouragement do

you need? Ask for it. How might you share it in faith to heal someone else?

7. What other scriptural passages sing the Birch Tree Song? Look here as a start: Numbers 20:16, Psalm 4.

CHAPTER 2

GATHER THE FRAGMENTS

*For moments of hunger
and abundance*

SCRIPTURAL GROUNDING
AND INSPIRATION

John 6: 1–13

After this Jesus went to the other side of the Sea of Galilee, also called the Sea of Tiberias. A large crowd kept following him, because they saw the signs that he was doing for the sick. Jesus went up the mountain and sat down there with his disciples. Now the Passover, the festival of the Jews, was near. When he looked up and saw a large crowd coming towards him, Jesus said to Philip, "Where are we to buy bread for these people to eat?" He said this to test him, for he himself knew what he was going to do. Philip answered him, "Six months' wages would not buy enough bread for each of them to get a little." One of his disciples, Andrew, Simon Peter's brother, said to him, "There is a boy here who has five barley loaves and two fish. But what are they among so many people?" Jesus said, "Make the people sit down." Now there was a great deal of grass in the place; so they sat down, about five thousand in all. Then Jesus took the loaves, and when he had given thanks, he distributed them to those who were seated; so also the fish, as much as they wanted. When they were satisfied, he told his disciples, "Gather up the fragments left over, so that nothing may be lost." So they gathered them up, and from the fragments of the five barley loaves, left by those who had eaten, they filled twelve baskets.

EXPERIENCE, STRENGTH, AND HOPE REFLECTION—EMBRACING THE MOMENT IN ALL OF CREATION

Grace was the theme at a women's retreat that I was helping facilitate. I was still using facilitation and leadership at that point in my own unlearning to keep my own vulnerable participation walled in a bit, but I was being led to be more open and to share. The retreat was at a large, old, stone monastery that lacked the warmth and coziness that some of the women craved. Discomfort is often a requirement of self-exploration, spiritual growth, and sharing, and there were parts of the physical environment that screamed that reality. I, however, love the old, cold, haunting monastery. I offered to sleep in a non-shared room on the third floor that was minimally heated in the Wisconsin January. I chose it because it had a cool (literally and figuratively) chapel next to the room where I could go to pray in solitude. I was graced to have this space to myself, graced to be hungry for prayer, and graced by the gratitude of others for my willingness to sleep there—grace in solitude, grace in gratitude, and grace in hunger.

The images of being hungry for God's grace, hungry for food, hungry, hungry, hungry for sustenance and healing are deeply present at the beginning of the Scriptural story of the feeding of the crowd. Also present is the teaching of going away, up the mountain, for a moment of retreat, when too many are seeking you for healing. Crowds of hungry seekers are always there, and retreating to the mountain was necessary, or at least a choice Jesus made, before action. These themes of hunger and withdrawing were the messages I was drawn to in the story when I was planning this retreat time, before I arrived there. Now on retreat, having placed myself in a cold solitary space "up the mountain" with Christ, I was led somewhere else.

I was led to the fragments left over after the feeding, to the abundance—to the *too much* to eat. God, through Jesus in this story, looks up at the crowd, meets us, sits us down, and feeds us— feeds us more that we can eat. Each moment is so abundant we cannot possibly take it all in for our hunger. God's Word, the presence and stories of others, warm blankets, shared song, creative opportunities, beautiful spaces, the outdoors, tasty food, silence, prayer, all these things were available in my moments on that women's retreat. Everything I need and more is right here, right now. I don't have room for it all. I was humbled by God's grace in the profound turning of my heart from hungry to abundantly full. I am reminded that I am not in charge. I must be willing to follow directions. I must sit down hungry, with humility, and be fed.

The messages of hunger and abundance have visited in many moments since that retreat. One day, my then seven year-old son said, somewhat dramatically as seven year old boys can be, "Mom, I am too starving to eat!" I was pushing carrots at that particular moment as he was headed hurriedly out the door with a ball in his hands, but it brought me right back to that retreat moment (thank goodness I was listening deeply). We are too tired to sleep, too hungry to taste, too blind to see, and maybe moving too fast aren't we? There is an abundance of gifts right before me all the time, in this moment, if I can only allow space for them. I must make space between my plans, my negative thinking, my belief that I am in charge, my worries of tomorrow, my obsession with yesterday, my problems, and my ego. My hunger and blindness are mine, and they lead me to seek God for help. God responds with grace-filled moments overflowing with blessings and abundance. It is I that has not room to taste and see. So I can only eat a bit, and whatever space I do have can be filled. I notice the fragments that fill twelve baskets are gathered up for later. Nothing will be lost. Grace and abundance wait for us in every moment.

MEDITATION AND PRAYER

To prepare for meditation and prayer time, sit still and first bring to your attention something you are grateful for. Spend a few moments, even a few minutes if you can, breathing this in and out. Next, bring to your attention a moment when you felt completely filled up. Spend a few moments breathing that in and out. Now, bring to your attention a moment where you felt hunger or longing. Attend to that feeling, too, for a few breaths. Finally, bring to your attention a past moment where you thought you were lacking or hungry, when, in retrospect, you realize that you were being fed more than you could see at the time. Know that truth in all moments. Sit quietly or walk quietly in that reality. Notice how this truth changes your perception of what is around and within you. There is more than enough. You are enough. God's love is abundant for you and for all. Consider starting and ending each day with a list of things you are grateful for, and if you ever have a chance, hold a newborn baby. Amen.

THE HEALING SONG OF NOW
GATHER THE FRAGMENTS

Find a quiet place to listen to the song, *Gather the Fragments.* Read or sing along with the song. Make no judgments about how you are participating in the song. Your voice and the way music moves in you is beautiful and is enough. Notice which parts of the song call out to you and linger there. Feel the words and the music drawing you to a place that needs healing, growth, or exploration.

Lyrics to *Gather the Fragments*

Gather the fragments; can you do it for me?
Pick up all the pieces of love that you see.
They're lying here broken, cast down on the ground.
I did not have room the first time they came round.

Gather the fragments of bread broken for me.
Space inside was too small, my eyes too blind to see.
They wait here in baskets, these gifts of Your grace
for hunger to trust, and my soul larger space

to claim all the fragments lying here on the ground,
to see the abundance, to know I am found.
Your eyes raised to mine and to know that it's true
I'm fed daily by fragments of love given by You.

QUESTIONS FOR THE MOMENT

1. Who is seeking you out for healing and care? What might *retreating to the mountain* to take care of yourself and your relationship with God before responding to other's needs look like to you?

2. In what ways or for what are you seeking and hungry? Where are you looking to be fed? What are you doing? Who are you asking for help? How might you respond to your hunger and seeking by sitting down and waiting to be fed?

3. Consider your attitude towards hunger. Do you see scarcity or abundance? There were twelve baskets left over after feeding the crowd. Make a list of twelve things for which you are grateful. These can be simple things like a cup of coffee and a smile from a stranger or big things like family, health, and a relationship with God. Return to your list and list-making

whenever you feel there is hunger or perceptions of not having enough. Reflect on the discipline of gratitude.

4. When have you felt seen by God? Were you hungry at the time? What happened? How do you define giving and receiving grace? How might you share experiences of grace with others?

5. Reflect on how much room you have to receive grace, healing, and love. What fragments of love have you cast aside? Where are they gathered? Who gathered them? Do you trust that they are not lost?

6. Reflect on extending grace, healing, and love to others and on whether they have room to receive them. What fragments of love have you given that have been cast aside? Do you trust God that these fragments are not to be lost? What stands in your way of trusting the abundance of each moment?

7. How does the song of the fragments help you heal and grow?

8. What is stirring in you as a response to the moment? Do you have a creative call or something stronger to write a poem, paint a picture, do a dance, or sing a new song? Do you feel a nudge to take a walk, sit in silence, talk to a friend, or start some new venture? Try it. What encouragement do you need? Ask for it. How might you share it in faith to heal someone else?

9. What other Scriptural passages sing the Gather the Fragments song? Look here as a start: Mark 8, John 21:4-6, Psalm 104.

HARVEST

For moments of emptying
and fruitfulness

SCRIPTURAL GROUNDING
AND INSPIRATION

Isaiah 18: 1-7

Ah, land of whirring wings beyond the rivers of Ethiopia, sending am-
bassadors by the Nile in vessels of papyrus on the waters! Go, you swift
messengers, to a nation tall and smooth, to a people feared near and
far, a nation mighty and conquering, whose land the rivers divide. All
you inhabitants of the world, you who live on the earth, when a signal
is raised on the mountains, look! When a trumpet is blown, listen! For
thus the Lord said to me: I will quietly look from my dwelling like clear
heat in sunshine, like a cloud of dew in the heat of harvest. For before
the harvest, when the blossom is over and the flower becomes a ripening
grape, he will cut off the shoots with pruning hooks, and the spreading
branches he will hew away. They shall all be left to the birds of prey of
the mountains and to the animals of the earth. And the birds of prey will
summer on them, and all the animals of the earth will winter on them.

At that time gifts will be brought to the Lord of hosts from a people tall and smooth, from a people feared near and far, a nation mighty and conquering, whose land the rivers divide, to Mount Zion, the place of the name of the Lord of hosts.

EXPERIENCE, STRENGTH, AND HOPE REFLECTION—EMBRACING THE MOMENT IN ALL OF CREATION

"Ah, land of whirring wings." That is my life and my thoughts some days, whirring from one place to another. I can almost hear the whir, the buzz, here and there, here and there, faster, faster, fly, fly, fly! *"When a signal is raised on the mountains, look! When a trumpet is blown, listen!"* Today is a day of retreat. This is a moment of retreat. Now is a moment to pay attention. *Look! Listen!* What do you see? What do you hear? I began my retreat at lunch with the sisters at the monastery I was visiting. *Listen!* One of the sisters thought she recognized me and during introductions, she asked me, "Aren't you an author?" I was not, at that point, an author, but certainly knew the creative call was being raised. *Listen!* I grinned at her as I was enjoying the return again to those first moments of retreat when the whirring slows and I can hear the whisper of the moment's song. "Maybe I am an author," I giggled inside but replied, "I am a writer, but I don't believe I am who you think I am." *Listen! Look!*

After lunch, I walked in the *clear heat in sunshine* all around the monastery grounds—among the pines, onto the prairie, up through the oaks, and then down to the wetland in conversation with the Scripture verse and the fullness of the earth in my moment. It was late fall. The apples hung heavy on the trees in the orchard. There was fall clean-up work being done—an emptying around the grounds—branches being cut away, cleared, hewn. *"For before the harvest, when the blossom is over and the flower becomes a ripening grape, he will cut off the shoots with pruning hooks, and the spreading branches he will hew away. They shall all be left to the birds of prey of the mountains and to the animals of the earth. And the birds of prey will summer on them, and all the animals of the earth will winter on them."* Oh how creation and Scripture speak the same truths. What was I to see in this? *Look!* What was I to hear in this? *Listen!* A snake slithered—*whirred*—through the grass in front of my step on the path and the milkweed stood full, tough, and ready to pop open and give the seeds to the wind. I walked past another apple tree that was heavy with fruit, yet had sprung new leaves still growing on the warm fall day. I tore a new leaf right off that tree like I had a pruning hook. *Look! Listen!* I saw a giant limb of a tree that had been hewn away by the grounds crew. It lay down on the earth with its many branches and leaves—birds and other creatures hopping about in it. Perhaps it could be a winter nest for one or two of them. The harvest is coming. The fruits are the focus. The rest is being emptied—cut away. I returned to the apple tree whose branches hung heavy with fruit. I dropped to my hands and knees, crawled beneath its branches, and found a small space to sit, to pray, to meditate—to be still within God. There is no other way to approach the emptying of the harvest, the cutting away of the new, and the fruits that are present, but on hands and knees.

The fruits are the focus. I must ask, what is the fruit of the moment right now? What is the singleness of purpose? From that walk, that Scripture, and in the silent, humble moment beneath the apple tree, I heard a focus on God as the fruit, not all those other things growing and branching that we whir and buzz around. There is nothing inherently wrong with those things. They may provide shelter for other creatures, but they are to be cut away to do so. The focus, the fruit, of this moment is the centrality of God and God's will for me. That focus is an empty focus—emptied of whirring and buzzing and branching—before the harvest, before the death of this moment. There is nothing else there, no branch—no new shoots—nothing to shield our attention from the fruits of the Spirit in this moment of harvest. In the moment right before the harvest, before the death, what is there to whir about, to finish, to branch, or to shoot?

Hear the trumpet sound. Pay attention. Get rid of the extraneous whirring for this moment. Let it be. Others will take it and use it. Trust in God and bear God's fruits of love and compassion and notice the beautiful emptiness around it all.

MEDITATION AND PRAYER

After some time in the stillness of meditation with God, I invite you to an outdoor walking meditation on God *"like clear heat in sunshine, like a cloud of dew in the heat of harvest."* Wherever you are walking, imagine a cloud of dew settled over the entire landscape or feeling a clear heat in sunshine on all that is. There is no place that a cloud of dew or clear heat doesn't touch. Approach this with humbleness and awe, but also in deep communion and conversation with God, the great Creator. So it is in the presence of God. All is touched, covered, and present. Take your steps slowly, and notice God is laid across all. Look! Listen! God is speaking to you in all of it. Can you find a place to drop to hands and knees, crawl beneath, and sit with God in the fruit of this moment? Amen.

THE HEALING SONG OF NOW
HARVEST

Find a quiet place to listen to the song, *Harvest*. Read or sing along with the song. Make no judgments about how you are participating in the song. Your voice and the way music moves in you is beautiful, and God is in it all. Notice which parts of the song call out to you and linger there. Feel the words and the music drawing you to place that needs healing, growth, or exploration.

Lyrics to *Harvest*

An emptiness precedes the harvest
in a space that draws summer to fall.
All stripped away, no room to say
can't say nothing, no, nothing at all.
The *I* meets us there in the branches
and the shoots that must be cut away.
For birds and for beasts to do what they will,
we're left only the fruits of today.

That's the space before the harvest we face
a space where so much don't belong.
In these wide open spaces, an emptiness graces
the moments before the harvest is gone.

A cloud of dew settles over the prairie,
fruits hanging low on the trees.
There's a space to sit under bowed down on the ground.
Come humble, on hands and on knees.
Raindrops fall to ground in the sunlight
as the wind blows them down from their beds.
Caught by the leaves then ripped from their dreams
for the harvest is coming instead.

That's the space before the harvest we face,
a space where so much don't belong.
In these wide open spaces, an emptiness graces
the moments before the harvest is gone.

Golden grasses lean tall towards the sun
whether rising or setting, the same.
Reaching out for the call to empty it all,
to lay down all, all but your name.
The wind has a bite of its own.
Yellows and purples won't rest.
Red's on the maple. Soup's on the table.
I've tears for the years in my chest.

Snakes slither by
the birds take to the sky
doing things that I did yesterday
before the emptiness called
the summer to fall
made the space that looms large round it all.

That's the space before the harvest we face,
a space where so much don't belong.
In these wide open spaces, an emptiness graces
the moments before the harvest is gone.

QUESTIONS FOR THE MOMENT

1. How is your life filled with the whirring of wings? What are the branches and shoots of your life in this moment? How important are they? If it all ended today, if the harvest came, what would be the fruit? Each moment comes to an end, what is the fruit of this moment?

2. How is the trumpet sounding the harvest in your life? What is the will of God calling you to be in this moment of retreat? What whirring needs to be stilled—what space cleared or emptied—in order to attend to the call of God?

3. God is laid across your life and all of creation like a cloud of dew. How might you surrender your will to that reality? How does that affect your pace? Your perspective? Your attention?

4. The song makes references to fall images like tall grasses, fruit trees, prairie, and wind. What are your images of fall or of harvest? The song makes references to fall colors: gold, yellow, red, and purple. What are your fall colors? There is even a reference to the comforts of soup followed by the weight of tears held in the heart in the fall. How does the comingling of this warm comfort and heavy sadness affect you in the light of God laid across it all? What emptying do you need to do?

5. How does the song of the harvest help you heal and grow?

6. What is stirring in you as a response to the moment? Do you have a creative call or something stronger to write a poem, paint a picture, do a dance, or sing a new song? Do you feel a nudge to take a walk, sit in silence, talk to a friend, or start some new venture? Try it. What encouragement do you need? Ask for it. How might you share it in faith to heal someone else?

7. What other Scriptural passages sing the Harvest song? Look here as a start: John 15, John 4: 34–36, Psalm 19:6.

CHAPTER 4

THE GOOD
SAMARITAN

For moments of
mercy and surprise

SCRIPTURAL GROUNDING
AND INSPIRATION

Luke 10: 25–37

Just then a lawyer stood up to test Jesus. 'Teacher,' he said, 'what must I do to inherit eternal life?' He said to him, 'What is written in the law? What do you read there?' He answered, "You shall love the Lord your God with all your heart, and with all your soul, and with all your strength, and with all your mind; and your neighbor as yourself." And he said to him, "You have given the right answer; do this, and you will live." But wanting to justify himself, he asked Jesus, "And who is my neighbor?" Jesus replied, "A man was going down from Jerusalem to Jericho, and fell into the hands of robbers, who stripped him, beat him, and went away, leaving him half dead. Now by chance a priest was going down that road; and when he saw him, he passed by on the other side. So likewise a Levite, when he came to the place and saw him, passed by on the other side. But a Samaritan while traveling came near him; and when he saw him, he was moved with pity. He went to him and bandaged his wounds, having poured oil and wine on them. Then he put him on his own animal, brought him to an inn, and took care of him. The next day he took out two denarii, gave them to the innkeeper, and said, 'Take care of him; and when I come back, I will repay you whatever more you spend.' Which of these three, do you think, was a neighbor to the man who fell into the hands of the robbers?" He said, "The one who showed him mercy." Jesus said to him, "Go and do likewise."

EXPERIENCE, STRENGTH, AND HOPE REFLECTION—EMBRACING THE MOMENT IN ALL OF CREATION

It is cold and dark as I arrive at a late-winter women's retreat in rural Wisconsin. By late winter in this part of the world, the coldness and darkness have become part of us—have settled into our very beings in a seemingly hopeless and eternal way. Creation is gray, empty, and ugly as the filth from the long winter sits atop icy piles of remaining snowbanks on frozen mud. I feel part of the ugliness. It is not a stretch to contemplate being beaten and in need of mercy. In this moment of retreat, with this familiar winter feeling and gospel story, that is where I identify myself—lying, beaten, on the side of the road. I can explain very little in the darkness that is in and around me, but I know that I am looking for light and mercy and spring. I am looking for mercy in the form of en*courage*ment—someone to put some *courage* in me. In my state, however, I don't have a lot of choice about from where or from whom it will come.

It seems I must explore this condition of being beaten. I am, fortunately, not reflecting on being physically beaten although I certainly hold in my heart those who have been. There are many. I am exploring more a sense of being beaten by life circumstances, patterns of living, disease, even death, and by the mess we find ourselves in sometimes. What does it mean to me to be beaten? Is it true that I have been *living in the hands of robbers*, robbers within and without, and what has been stolen from me? Is this just a game I have been beaten at—a game of strategy, power, manipulation, or chance? What part of the loss belongs to me? How have I beaten myself—stolen my own joy, serenity, or self-worth? What part belongs to others? How have others beaten me—manipulated, misused, excluded, or devalued my gifts, and how is it that I chose to be playing the game with them? These cold and dark questions, like filthy snowbanks on frozen mud, fill me with a certain despair that contains sadness and, I must claim it—*anger.* I am beaten, sad, and angry. I am in need of mercy.

Stay inside—go inside—stay inside where it is not cold and dark. There is a whisper from a previously untouched place inside of me, a warmer, lighter place that says, "Help me." It calls first to the sources that I believe will help, that I believe *should* help, that have helped, historically—the priest, the Levite, and others, like them. They walk by. They can't help me. Their systems, their ways, their rules, their busy-ness—they are not equipped to help. But they are part of the story—part of the teaching. Perhaps, I am too bloody, vulnerable, and exposed—*stripped* too naked. Like Peter at the cross, they betray, for reasons non known or controllable. I am changing, my systems are changing, and tensions and risks seem high. I am cold in the darkness in the ugly late winter, and even though I feel abandoned and alone, I somehow still trust that God has not walked by. Beneath the snow pile, there is always a sleeping, surprising spring. God always surprises. It is true for me in this moment, too. I receive help from a surprising source, a *foreign* source, a *Samaritan* source. I am surprised. It is mercy.

This help, this foreign mercy, is sacred. It comes in the form of encouragement from a new spiritual community with traditions of non-judgment, safety, and healing. It comes from old, thought lost, friends who encourage me to find and reclaim the music and beauty they knew in me as a child. It comes from existing friends or acquaintances that are willing to risk newness and change to explore healing, growth, and the messiness of the process. They encourage. They *bandage my wounds.* They *pour oil and wine.* The cost of my care is in time and energy and their risk to love. It is expensive, and I value it. I begin to heal, and I touch and explore that warm place of light, that foreign whispering place *inside* of me. A voice from there emerges like a surprising spring, first shaky, but centered and rooted, and, then, louder and blossoming. From that foreign place within, I voice, in song, that I *am* going to reclaim what has been stolen. I will heal and reclaim joy, serenity, and self-worth. I will do the work. It is mercy. The road is filled with surprise.

The steps further down the road do require work and surprising new things of me. The encouragement and mercy that I received demand a larger view from me of God's presence in the world—a view beyond the walls of the church or any other sacred institution and also from new and humbler places within those walls. My attitude and perspective on the merciful role that encouragement plays in healing is new and foreign but welcome and deeply life-giving. I learn how to encourage myself. I develop daily disciplines of journaling, prayer and meditation, and gratitude. *I make and celebrate mistakes, and I don't beat myself up.* I write, write, and write some more. I buy a guitar. I take voice lessons. I encourage myself. *I make mistakes, and I don't beat myself up.* I stop chasing the *"shoulds"* and try accepting help from the new, surprising spring. I create, record, and release two CDs of songs that came from within me. Surprise! I title the CDs *She Stands* and *Into the Light* to claim the journey of standing up after being beaten and of listening to the foreign light within. I write, write, and write some more to share the light, to share the mercy, and to encourage. I write a book. Surprise! I hope it heals. I encourage myself. *I make mistakes, and I don't beat myself up.* Now go, and do likewise.

MEDITATION AND PRAYER

This is a mindfulness meditation. During your day today and in your week ahead, notice whom you are kind and courteous to, and to whom you are not. Notice whom you ask to help you and whom you do not. As you increase your attention to this behavior, attempt a shift on an occasion. Ask someone for help whom you normally would not ask for help. Notice what happens. Attempt courtesy or kindness toward someone you normally would not show it toward. As you do this, ask God to show you mercy and to give you courage to show mercy to others no matter what the cost. Compassion and mercy shared on the road go a long way to healing ourselves and the world. Be open to surprise. Amen.

THE HEALING SONG OF NOW
THE GOOD SAMARITAN

Find a quiet place to listen to the song, *The Good Samaritan*. Read or sing along with the song. Make no judgments about how you are participating in the song. Your voice and the way music moves in you is beautiful and merciful even if it feels foreign. Notice which parts of the song call out to you, and linger there. Feel the words and the music drawing you to a place that needs healing, growth, or exploration.

Lyrics to *The Good Samaritan*

Oh, they beat me and cast me aside.
I was cowering bleeding and blind.
On the road out of town,
I laid myself down.
I laid down and waited to die.

And you didn't help me.
No, you stayed far away from me
watching me bleed
watching me need.
Now you stand there so righteously
like it was a choice for me.
It wasn't a choice, you see.
I didn't choose
who would take mercy.
Mercy, take mercy.
Lord, who would take mercy on me.

Oh, my holy and learned passed by.
From my nakedness, they shielded their eyes.
The followers too
oh, I think I saw you
cast a glance but cling tight to the line.

And you didn't help me.
No you stayed far away from me
watching me bleed,
watching me need.
Now, you stand there so righteously
like it was a choice for me.
It wasn't a choice, you see.
I didn't choose
who would take mercy.

Mercy, take mercy.
Lord, who would take mercy on me.

From a place that I dared not to dream,
a foreigner, she fell to her knees.
She gathered me in,
risked love for my sin.
It was mercy.
She showed mercy on me.

And you didn't help me.
No, you stayed far away from me
watching me bleed,
watching me need.
Now you stand there so righteously
like it was a choice for me.
It wasn't a choice, you see.
I didn't choose
who would take mercy.
Mercy, take mercy.
Lord, who would take mercy on me.

QUESTIONS FOR THE MOMENT

1. When have you felt like you were beaten and could not help yourself? What was it like to be that vulnerable—that needy? Name your emotions, even if they aren't pretty. Who or what picked you up? If you have been *picked up* from a Samaritan or foreign place inside or outside yourself that surprised you, how did you feel? How did others react? How did your relationships with God and others change? What was the cost of your care (financial, emotional, in time)?

2. Reflect on an experience when either you or someone else did not offer help, encouragement, or mercy in a time of need. Reflect on the Priest and the Levite and who or what these

people might represent in your own experience. Who is the foreigner, the Samaritan, in you that picks you up? How do you see the foreign places within, as sacred places to embrace gently and with gratitude or do you fear them or judge them harshly? Why? Notice—does that occur on the outside, as well, when you encounter something foreign?

3. What helps you to or keeps you from seeing God in all of your experiences? Have you ever been surprised to be called to pick someone else up? Reflect on that time or experience. How does this change your understanding of God?

4. All these characters in the story ultimately play a role in mercy being granted and healing to occur. Considering that larger picture, explore how healing has occurred in your life? How does it inform what you might be facing in this moment? Are you in a spiritual community as a leader or follower that is watching someone in need? How can you show encouragement or mercy in a new or foreign way to this person? To yourself? What, if any, is the role of forgiveness in this story?

5. What is it like for you to ask for help? Whom do you ask? Are there people you don't ask for help? Why? How do you offer help to others? Are there times you have not offered help to someone? Why or why not? Was healing affected? What is it that calls you to offer help? Try incorporating a discipline of intentional acts of kindness and help during your day and reflect on the experience.

6. How does the meditation and song of the Good Samaritan help you heal and grow?

7. What is stirring in you as a response to the moment? Do you have a creative call—or something stronger—to write a poem, paint a picture, do a dance, or sing a new song? Do you feel a nudge to take a walk, sit in silence, talk to a friend, or start some new venture? Try it. What encouragement do

you need? Ask for it. How might you share it in faith to heal someone else?

8. What other Scriptural passages sing the Good Samaritan song? Look here as a start: Mark 9:38–50, Numbers 11.

CHAPTER 5

THE NARROWS

*For moments of circling
and perseverance*

SCRIPTURAL GROUNDING
AND INSPIRATION

Second Esdras 7: 3–5

I said, "Speak, my lord." And he said to me, "There is a sea set in a wide expanse so that it is deep and vast, but it has an entrance set in a narrow place, so that it is like a river. If there are those who wish to reach the sea, to look at it or to navigate it, how can they come to the broad part unless they pass through the narrow part?"

2 Samuel 14:14 (CEV)

We each must die and disappear like water poured out on the ground. But God doesn't take our lives. Instead he figures out ways of bringing us back when we run away.

EXPERIENCE, STRENGTH, AND HOPE
REFLECTION—EMBRACING THE
MOMENT IN ALL OF CREATION

This journey of the narrows began on a personal retreat where I was feeling pressed. I felt squeezed into narrow spots—squeezed by narrow thinking, by over-thinking, and by judgment in places where I expected gentleness and encouragement. I felt limited by the pace of learning, the pace of healing, and I perceived a lack of forward progress, a circling around the same issues over and over, and a general dissatisfaction with the place I stood on my path.

I found myself in conversation with the 2 Edras reading at a retreat location that manifested my inner condition in the outer surroundings—a place of twisting streams, narrow pathways, and labyrinths. Many retreat centers have labyrinths, pathways that circle around and around, arriving at a center. I have walked many labyrinths and have experienced them, again and again, as wonderfully meditative and reflective encounters with myself, with God, and with others and the world. In this moment, I forced a slow walk through the stone path labyrinth that was set on a cliff overlooking Lake Michigan, and I gently touched a truth of the reading—that in order to enter the sea, we must *pass through the narrow part*. This takes time, readiness, willingness, grace, and perseverance. The message of that walk was, *"keep walking."* As I circled around and around, it sometimes seemed as if I was getting nowhere at all, but I had to notice the truth, that each spot is always in a slightly different place. I am someplace new, narrow or not, and I trust that the steps I continue to take are leading me to the sea—that expanse of freedom. For a long time, I thought that freedom was reaching the center of the labyrinth and some center in me. But that *expanse* expanded—in time.

In the years that followed that retreat, the teaching of perseverance towards center spilled into most of my moments—spilled, like water. I spent much time seeing and accepting the squeeze—the many narrows—the paths, the twisting streams, the blades of knife—as the path or the means to arriving at center. And like walking the labyrinth, my perseverance rewarded me with a discovery of center—a freedom, a truth, a love of self—true self—a resting in and knowing God within. The disciplines of trusting and persevering—requiring only one step at a time, one day at a time, one moment at a time—kept me walking, circling, and carried me to a center filled with love. Then, one day, I was in a new moment of retreat in the mossy, mountain forests of Oregon walking another labyrinth, and I realized that I was no longer walking into center, but back out again, and, surprisingly, I still felt free.

I thought the journey was in, that the final step into the freedom of the sea was reaching center, but I have found that we are called also to wind our way back out to the others. God finds a way to call us, to *bring us back*, freely, in both directions. Like *water poured on the ground*, I had run my way in, but God finds a way to bring us back, to circle the water back out just like the cycle of all water in creation circles. The journey of the narrows and of the labyrinth is the *circling in* and the *circling out*, over and over again.

Over and over, we persevere in taking the fruits of a still center out into the world and then taking the tumult and waves of the world back into center to love all of it. I even began to consider each breath a labyrinth into center and back out again. Exhale—love drawing me, calling me, *bringing* me back in to a still lake, to center. Inhale—love pushing me, driving me, *bringing* me back out to the sea. How does God call us back and forth? After I walked out of that mossy, mountain labyrinth, slowly and intentionally, I went and sat in a naturally fed steam sauna at the retreat center (yes, you should be jealous). In it was a man singing songs about water and rivers, and my voice leapt in and joined without hesitation. It was then that I named one way that that God brings *me* back and forth, from within to without—from lake to sea—from exhale to inhale. Like *water poured on the ground*, I am called to join a river of song that flows and circles between lake and sea—free.

MEDITATION AND PRAYER

If you have an opportunity, find a narrow place to walk that winds along a stream, loops, or circles, or, even better, find a labyrinth in your community or a nearby retreat center. Consider the narrow path that you must walk, and how you must journey to center and back out again. Before you start, exhale love as you circle into your center. Imagine God drawing you or bringing you into God's self. Then inhale love as you circle yourself out to the world. Imagine God blowing you, pushing you, like an instrument being filled and sent into the world. After that cleansing breath, read the poem below and then start your walk. *Walk, walk, walk the narrows.* When you reach center, inhale love and exhale love, and then read the poem again. Slowly walk back out of the labyrinth and spend some time with your breath, in prayer, or journaling.

Water Poured on the Ground
A Prayer of Circling to Center and Return

I hid in the spin
and the swirl of the sea
bound and true.
The journey to there
taught me to care
for you, for you
and to love
and to do.

Then a voice called me round to the center
found a way to turn me around,
and I disappeared slowly
as death called me down
to the lake where I ran
like water poured onto the ground.

I hid in the calm
and the depths of the lake
found and free.
The journey to there
taught me to care
for me, for me
and to love
and to be.

Then a voice called me round to the edge
found a way to turn me around,
and I disappeared slowly
as death called me out
to the sea where I ran
like water poured onto the ground.

The way that I ran was a spiral
between the lake and sea.
Over and over
the water was poured,
and I ran between you and me.
It became a river of song
heavy with droplets of steam.
The lake became you
the sea became me.
All was doing.
All was being.
All was seen.
All was lost.
All was found.
All was song
in the steam.
All is love
in between
round and round
round and round
as water is poured on the ground.

THE HEALING SONG OF NOW
THE NARROWS

Find a quiet place to listen to the song, *The Narrows*. Read or sing along with the song. Make no judgments about how you are participating in the song. Your voice and the way music moves in you is beautiful and carries you along your path as much as your feet do. Notice which parts of the song call out to you and linger there. Feel the words and the music drawing you to a place that needs healing, growth, or exploration.

Lyrics to *The Narrows*

Walk, walk, walk the narrows,
walk the narrows to the sea.
The narrows narrow, I beg for arrows
each step I make with me.
So I walk, walk, walk the narrows,
walk the narrows to the sea.

A narrow crack,
a twisting stream,
a blade of knife cuts me clean.
Birth canal,
pulsing veins,
narrowed eyes search my name, as I

walk, walk, walk the narrows,
walk the narrows to the sea.
The narrows narrow, rage and barrel,
but the current runs with me
as I walk, walk, walk the narrows
walk the narrows to the sea.

A narrow street,
a string that rings,
air that stands beneath the wings.
Chapel pews,
gasping breath,
narrow escapes from thoughtful death, as I

walk, walk, walk the narrows
walk the narrows to the sea.

The labyrinth,
the walls of caves,
needles piercing skin to save.
Body standing,
still and whole,
a narrow passage to the soul, so I

walk, walk, walk the narrows,
walk the narrows to the sea.
The narrows narrow, I beg for arrows,
and then one step we're free, so I
walk, walk, walk the narrows,
walk the narrows to the sea.

QUESTIONS FOR THE MOMENT

1. What narrow places do you find yourself in today? How might the image of circling into a lake or sea of center help you in accepting these spots and continuing to walk? What encouragement do you need to persevere? How do you practice living life just one day at a time—one step at a time?

2. In what ways are you stuck or finding that you have stopped walking the path? How can you start again? How does God call you to continue the journey? Through writing, song,

family, painting, walking, prayer, something else? How might you listen and respond to that call today?

3. Reflect in the image of the labyrinth with the center being a still lake within you and the outer edge being the sea of others and the world. Where do you spend most of your time and energy, the lake or sea? If you have run too far or too long in one direction, how is God calling you to shift your orientation? What does God's bringing you back look, sound, or feel like?

4. Are you hiding in self or in others, within or without, and if so, what are you hiding from?

5. What does your breath teach you about circling in and out? What does it teach you about perseverance?

6. How does the prayer and song of the narrows help you heal and grow?

7. What is stirring in you as a response to the moment? Do you have a creative call—or something stronger—to write a poem, paint a picture, do a dance, or sing a new song? Do you feel a nudge to take a walk, sit in silence, talk to a friend, or start some new venture? Try it. What encouragement do you need? Ask for it. How might you share it in faith to heal someone else?

8. What other Scriptural passages sing The Narrows song? Look here to start: Psalm 16:11, Matthew 7:13 – 14, Luke 13:24.

Warrior
Angel

*God of dreams and intuition, give
me faith that you will guide my
choices with your wisdom.* Amen

CHAPTER 6

UNKNOWING

*For moments of
mystery and trust*

SCRIPTURAL GROUNDING
AND INSPIRATION

John 9: 1–41

As he walked along, he saw a man blind from birth. His disciples asked him, "Rabbi, who sinned, this man or his parents, that he was born blind?" Jesus answered, "Neither this man nor his parents sinned; he was born blind so that God's works might be revealed in him. We must work the works of him who sent me while it is day; night is coming when no one can work. As long as I am in the world, I am the light of the world." When he had said this, he spat on the ground and made mud with the saliva and spread the mud on the man's eyes, saying to him, "Go, wash in the pool of Siloam" (which means Sent). Then he went and washed and came back able to see. The neighbors and those who had seen him before as a beggar began to ask, "Is this not the man who used to sit and beg?" Some were saying, "It is he." Others were saying, "No, but it is someone like him." He kept saying, "I am the man." But they kept asking him, "Then how were your eyes opened?" He answered, "The man called Jesus made mud, spread it on my eyes, and said to me, 'Go to Siloam and wash.' Then I went and washed and received my sight." They said to him, "Where is he?" He said, "I do not know." They brought to the Pharisees the man who had formerly been blind. Now it was a sabbath day when Jesus made the mud and opened his eyes. Then the Pharisees also began to ask him how he had received his sight. He said to them, "He put mud on my eyes. Then I washed, and now I see." Some of the Pharisees said, "This man is not from God, for he does not observe the sabbath." But others said, "How can a man who is a sinner perform such signs?" And they were divided. So they said again to the blind man, "What do you say about him? It was your eyes he opened." He said, "He is a prophet." The Jews did not believe that he had been blind and had received his sight until they called the parents of the man who had received his sight and asked them, "Is this your son, who you say was born blind? How then does he now see?" His parents answered, "We know that this is our son, and that he was born blind; but we do not know how it is that now he sees, nor do we know who opened his eyes. Ask him; he is of age. He will speak for himself." His parents said this because they were afraid of the Jews; for the Jews had already agreed that anyone who confessed Jesus to be the Messiah would be put out of the synagogue. Therefore his parents said, "He is of age; ask him." So for the second time they called the man who had been blind, and they said to him, "Give glory to God! We know that this man is a sinner." He answered, "I do not know whether he is a sinner. One thing I do know, that though I was blind, now I see." They said to him, "What did he do to you? How did he open your eyes?" He answered them, "I have told you already, and you would not listen. Why do you want to hear it again? Do you also want to become his disciples?" Then they reviled him, saying, "You are his disciple, but we are disciples of Moses. We know that God has spoken to Moses, but as for this man, we do not know where he comes from." The man answered, "Here is an astonishing thing! You do not know where he comes from, and yet he opened my eyes. We know that God does not listen to sinners, but he does listen to one who worships him and obeys his will. Never since the world began has it been heard that anyone opened the eyes of a person born blind. If this man were not from God, he could do nothing." They answered him, "You were born entirely in sins, and are you trying to teach us?" And they drove him out. Jesus heard that they had driven him out, and when he found him, he said, "Do you believe in the Son of Man?" He answered, "And who is he, sir? Tell me, so that I may believe in him." Jesus said to him, "You have seen him, and the one speaking with you is he." He said, "Lord, I believe." And he worshiped him. Jesus said, "I came into this world for judgment so that those who do not see may see, and those who do see may become blind." Some of the Pharisees near him heard this and said to him, "Surely we are not blind, are we?" Jesus said to them, "If you were blind, you would not have sin. But now that you say, 'We see,' your sin remains."

EXPERIENCE, STRENGTH, AND HOPE REFLECTION—EMBRACING THE MOMENT IN ALL OF CREATION

Unknowing seems to follow those who are paying attention. Unknowing used to cause me so much fear. It used to contribute to denial and to my behaviors of over-planning and attempts to control others. How often do we ask why? How often do we stand in judgment of a situation in order to protect our own order and perceptions so we don't have to face the reality of how little we know? And what about those times of awakening, where we do know, but we doubt? How often do we take that doubt to those outside of ourselves, the *experts* either by education or self-proclamation, to hear where we should go next?

The Scriptural story of unknowing goes on and on, doesn't it? Did you even read it all? Be honest. The moments for this retreat were just the same and seemed to go on and on and on and on. Isn't that the way we try to deal with the fear of the unknowing—talk, talk, talk, talk—push, push, push, push—ask around,

43

see what others are doing, try to prove someone else can't really see something they are clearly seeing (Haven't they always been blind?), try to direct those who have newly awakened or strayed from the ordered world that we have organized to keep ourselves safe? On and on and on we go.

I was practicing living my moments of retreat, my moments of deep listening, in my regular day to day activities rather than protected at a retreat center for the week. The song, the words, the messages of unknowing whispered to me in a chapel worship service during which the passage of scripture was read. I had been watching the river in my neighborhood closely that week and had been wondering what the water would say to me about the journey. Water flows. That is it: water flows. Does it know where it will be? Perhaps it will be sustenance for the roots of the willow tree that grows there or quench the thirst of the bird that nests in the willow. Perhaps it will find its way around the bend. The truth is that it doesn't know. We are the same, like water, of water, from water, born of water, and flowing. We don't know either. We don't know the reason, the season, what impact our action or inaction will have in this moment or will have in the future. And yet, this rubs me wrong. Don't I have control over this? Am I not in charge? If I purchase this, study this, learn this, follow these rules, make you happy, fix this, won't I be successful, happy, fulfilled, loved, worthy? So often in my life, I have let others define the right way for me—based upon *their* plans, *their* certainty, *their* ego, *their* illusion of knowing.

When music and poetry emerged in me, I was raw, shocked, delighted, and scared. I was the blind man with new sight. I knew God was healing me and that I had touched a little piece of *God's* will for my life. I also knew nothing else. I didn't know where I was going, whom I was to be helping, feeding, or healing, or who was supposed to be helping, feeding, and healing me. Like water in the river, I had to let it flow. I had to endure the questioning and the inquiry and the doubt from the Pharisees in my life, within and without, who always knew the answer, who sent me away as the blind-from-birth sinner, but who, in the end, were left questioning even themselves about whether they see or know.

God's healing power and the teachings of our lives are a mystery, ever so slowly shown by grace alone. We must trust our new sight when it is granted, accept that neither we nor others know where we are headed, and, with that trust, embrace the mystery of this moment of retreat, this moment of song, this moment on the river, humbly and on equal footing with all of creation. But by the grace of God, I am a witness to this moment, at this spot in the river of time. Isn't it a mystery to enjoy?

MEDITATION AND PRAYER

We can learn to experience the delight and joy in unknowing with a still and silent meditation practice. This is difficult in a society where we have been taught to be *crazy busy*, on the move, knowledgeable, and productive. There are many methods to meditation. For this moment of retreat, I suggest you try a mantra-based meditation practiced by John Main and by the World Community of Christian Meditation. Below is a short excerpt from those meditation and mantra teachings that have led me and many others, and may lead you, to a discipline of stilling your mind and being in deeper conscious contact with God.

What is Meditation

Open to all ways of wisdom but drawing directly from the early Christian teaching John Main summarized the practice in this simple way:

Sit down. Sit still with your back straight. Close your eyes lightly. Then interiorly, silently begin to recite a single word – a prayer word or mantra. We recommend the ancient Christian prayer-word "Maranatha". Say it as four equal syllables. Breathe normally and give your full attention to the word as you say it, silently, gently, faithfully and above all - simply. The essence of meditation is simplicity. Stay with the same word during the whole meditation and from day to day. Don't visualize but listen to the word as you say it. Let go of all thoughts (even good thoughts), images and other words. Don't fight your distractions but let them go by saying your word faithfully, gently and attentively and returning to it immediately that you realize you have stopped saying or it or when your attention is wandering.

Silence means letting go of thoughts. Stillness means letting go of desire. Simplicity means letting go of self-analysis.

Meditate twice a day every day. This daily practice may take you sometime to develop. Be patient. When you give up start again. You will find that a weekly meditation group and a connection with a community may help you develop this discipline and allow the benefits and fruits of meditation to pervade your mind and every aspect of your life in ways that will teach and delight you. John Main said that 'meditation verifies the truths of your faith in your own experience'.[1]

---

1 The World Community of Christian Meditation, "What is Meditation".

The Mantra

In the twentieth century John Main . . . recommended the early Aramaic Christian prayer 'maranatha'. This is a scriptural phrase meaning 'Come Lord' (1Cor: 16:22), in the language Jesus spoke, Aramaic, and a sacred phrase in the early Christian liturgy. There are many other examples of suggested prayer-words in the history of Christian prayer reflecting the particular epoch or the personality of the master of prayer who was leading others into contemplative silence and stillness (hesychia) in the heart. Common to the tradition is the emphasis on continuous repetition of the word with deepening faith and fidelity to the same word as it becomes rooted in the heart and opens the grace of contemplation – our entry into the prayer of Jesus himself in the Holy Spirit.[2]

THE HEALING SONG OF NOW
UNKNOWING

Find a quiet place to listen to the song, *Unknowing*. Read or sing along with the song. Make no judgments about how you are participating in the song. Your voice and the way music moves in you is beautiful, and it is not necessary to understand it or judge it. Notice which parts of the song call out to you and linger there. Feel the words and the music drawing you to a place that needs healing, growth, or exploration.

2 The World Community of Christian Meditation, "The Mantra".

Lyrics to *Unknowing*

If you're water in the river, do you know?
Are you certain you'll wash to the sea?
Would you know that the path lies
direct as the crow flies?
Would it speak like you're talking to me?

You know, you think that you're flowing;
you think that you're knowing;
the course is carved out, it's clearly downstream,
but you may be for sowing
the willow that's growing
or for the thirst of the bird, the bird or the bee.

If one day the blind man could see,
if he stood there and said how it was so,
would you scorn at his healing?
Would you judge his revealing?
Would you direct him to all that you know?

You know, you think that you're flowing;
you think that you're knowing;
the course is carved out, it's clearly downstream,
but you may be for sowing
the willow that's growing
or for the thirst of the bird, the bird or the bee.

Would the water say stay?
Would the water say go?
Would it say something more
than be where you flow?
Would it say that it's certain
to be round the bend?
or say there's just one way
to loving a friend?

No, you don't know the reason,
and you don't know the season.
You don't know the role that you play.
You don't know if you're flowing
where this river is going.
The truth
is in the *unknowing*
is all that the water would say.

QUESTIONS FOR THE MOMENT

1. What *why* questions are you turning over and over in your mind today? How much time and energy are they taking from this moment of retreat? How can you turn them over to God—trusting them to the river of unknowing?

2. When have you experienced an awakening of sight—a light in a previously blind situation? What was happening in your life? How have you tried to explain it? Might you have touched a little piece of God's will for you? What healing or clarity was given? What role does doubt play for you in following the new current?

3. Do you have a meditation practice? What resistance, if any, do you have to a discipline of meditation? How could you start or deepen your practice?

4. In what ways are you questioning how others see and experience things? Explore whether you are offering too much direction, trying to control outcomes for yourself or others, or calling on your own inner Pharisee and credentials to tell someone what they do or don't see. Reflect on whether you believe that you know what's best for others.

5. Where are you on the river today? What are you doing that may be sowing, quenching, healing, or moving? Can you

release your ideas and plans for where you or your loved ones are heading and simply witness what gifts exist is this moment? What does the word *mystery* mean to you? Can you accept that you don't know the way your actions today will affect any outcome around the bend? What does it require of you to *trust*?

6. Today, you are right where you are supposed to be. For what are you grateful? What is beautiful right now? Others find themselves in different circumstances. How can you honor those circumstances with the same gratitude and humility in the face of unknowing?

7. How does the song of unknowing help you heal and grow?

8. What is stirring in you as a response to the moment? Do you have a creative call—or something stronger—to write a poem, paint a picture, do a dance, or sing a new song? Do you feel a nudge to take a walk, sit in silence, talk to a friend, or start some new venture? Try it. What encouragement do you need? Ask for it. How might you share it in faith to heal someone else?

9. What other Scriptural passages sing the Unknowing song? Look here to start: John 3:8, Genesis 11, Acts 2.

CHAPTER 7

MILKWEED

*For moments of letting
go and acceptance*

SCRIPTURAL GROUNDING
AND INSPIRATION

Matthew 26: 36–44

Then Jesus went with them to a place called Gethsemane; and he said to his disciples, "Sit here while I go over there and pray." He took with him Peter and the two sons of Zebedee, and began to be grieved and agitated. Then he said to them, "I am deeply grieved, even to death; remain here, and stay awake with me." And going a little farther, he threw himself on the ground and prayed, "My Father, if it is possible, let this cup pass from me; yet not what I want but what you want." Then he came to the disciples and found them sleeping; and he said to Peter, "So, could you not stay awake with me one hour? Stay awake and pray that you may not come into the time of trial; the spirit indeed is willing, but the flesh is weak." Again he went away for the second time and prayed, "My Father, if this cannot pass unless I drink it, your will be done." Again he came and found them sleeping, for their eyes were heavy. So leaving them again, he went away and prayed for the third time, saying the same words.

EXPERIENCE, STRENGTH, AND HOPE REFLECTION—EMBRACING THE MOMENT IN ALL OF CREATION

Have you ever seen a milkweed plant? Those of us that live in the Midwest are graced by their presence in the fields and the prairies. They are a plant, in many ways, of transformation—being home and food for monarch caterpillars. The milkweed plant itself grows large pods that almost look like the large chrysalis of the monarch that lives on it. The pods start out small and green but grow and expand throughout the summer months until they are fat and bursting. In the late fall, bursting is what they do. They burst open, and hundreds of tiny seeds are released and let go, a seed at a time, to the wind like little white feathers flying to unknown destinations to plant new life again.

The song of the milkweed first sang to me in the fall when I had returned in walking prayer to the prairie garden like Christ, grappling with God's will for me. The fat, brown, milkweed pods on their stalks were ready to burst open and send their seeds out to the wind, and they asked me to let go, to let die, to let old self, old behaviors, old perceptions, and old expectations of myself and others go. Let them fly just like every living thing must, in the end, do—just like the milkweed plant reckons itself to the winds of fall and sends out all it has stored up inside.

There is fear. I don't want to let go of what was. I don't want to reckon with death. I fear. What do I fear—a loss of control, a break in denial and illusion, a claiming of loneliness and imperfection? What do I fear—the pain of healing, the transformation required in relationships with others, with work, with church, with friends, with family, with God? What do I fear—that I must change myself—stop pointing a finger outside at what is wrong with others and the world—their selfishness, their anger, their policies, their spiritual poverty—and look at how those very things are what is wrong in me? What do I fear—that I must rest in God's will and not by own, that I must be humble, that I must trust where death leads?

The milkweed and the garden of Gethsemane ask that I reckon with death sometimes in big ways. In one two-week period of my life, when I had returned again to singing with the *Milkweed* song, a colleague of mine at work lost her thirty-four-year-old daughter in a car crash, a friend of mine said goodbye to and lost her father to a stroke, and my daughter's school community lost an eleven-year-old boy in a train accident. Just three blocks from my home, her classmate was hit by a train on his walk to school. *Dead.* Reckoning was the message—reckoning with death. In the story from Gethsemane, I hear, *Must I drink this cup*? Jesus threw himself on the ground and prayed, *"My Father, if it is possible, let this cup pass from me; yet not what I want but what you want."* The Milkweed tells me that I have no choice but to crack open my heart and let all that is there go a seed at a time, in each moment, let it go into the hands of God's will. God's will, not mine, be done. I get to practice this letting go and acceptance over and over again.

Acceptance, letting go, and death are the words of the milkweed, yes, but what of freedom, transformation, and life? These too are the words of the milkweed. The truth is that we must die to live. Fall is necessary for the next spring. The caterpillar must die to emerge a butterfly. The seed must be released to grow anew. There is winter, of course, in between. Death, winter, a rest is needed, too, for growth. Death precedes resurrection. Our lives and our retreat moments so often require this reckoning and, ultimately, an acceptance of this cycle of the letting go, the rest or waiting, and the transformation or resurrection to new life. The reality of the milkweed is a reality that each moment calls us to practice. We have seeds hoarded up inside our hearts that are not ours to keep. Each breath, each smile, each prayer, each hello, each goodbye, each and every moment I give to God. There is freedom in this trust, in this rest, and this faith that there will be resurrection on the other side of letting go. That is the promise that Jesus fulfilled and taught us in the events after his prayers of acceptance and letting go in garden of Gethsemane.

MEDITATION AND PRAYER

To prepare for this meditation and prayer time, I invite you to locate a little piece of nature that can be used to let things go. What is available will depend upon what season you are in. If it is summer time, find a dandelion gone to seed or a flower with petals. If it is autumn, find a milkweed pod or a small stack of fallen leaves. If it is winter or spring, find a packet of seeds or something similar. Spend some time seated in silence with the item you have found and reflect on the cycle of letting go, rest, and new life. Ask that God use the milkweed pod, leaves, flower, or seeds to connect you to that cycle and to teach you how to accept and to let go. Make a mental or written list of people or situations that you are carrying heavily in your heart, are trying to control, or are worried about. Sit in silence with that list and with your object and ask God to hold it all, including you. When you are ready, go outdoors, and take a seed at a time, a leaf at a time, a petal at a time, a seed at a time, and release it to the wind. With each release, name a situation or person you are trying to let go, and offer a smile, a prayer, a name, and a goodbye, and let it go.

THE HEALING SONG OF NOW
MILKWEED

Find a quiet place to listen to the song, *Milkweed.* Read or sing along with the song. Make no judgments about how you are participating in the song. Your voice and the way music moves in you is beautiful and aids in your own reckoning. Notice which parts of the song call out to you and linger there. Feel the words and the music drawing you to a place that needs healing, growth, or exploration.

Lyrics to the *Milkweed Song*

Hardened and dry,
hoarding inside,
what delights in the light of the sun.
Holding on tight,
growing in might,
for a journey that has not begun.

I'm ready to die.
I'm ready to fly.
Like the fall
milkweed, I . . .

. . . broke open, let go,
just blow, blow,
float off to a place in the sky.
Maybe land once again
somewhere with no end,
no hoarding, no need for goodbye.

I'm ready to die.
I'm ready to fly.
like the fall
milkweed, I . . .

. . . open my heart.
Let love fly
a seed at a time, a seed at a time,
a smile at a time, an eye at a time,
a care at a time, prayer at a time,
goodbye at a time.

I'm ready to die.
I'm ready to fly.
like the fall
milkweed . . . I

QUESTIONS FOR THE MOMENT

1. With what death are you reckoning? Explore the fears you are experiencing? What stops you from going away to the garden as Christ did and laying your grief, confusion, and agitation before your God and humbling yourself to God's will? What does going to the garden look like for you—prayer, retreat, writing, conversation, song, quiet, a walk? Can you trust God's will as a place of certain rest, resurrection, and life?

2. What have you built up and grown inside your heart that needs to be released and let go? What would it be like to do it a little at a time, like a seed from a milkweed plant? What helps you see it as a release of love and a hope for new life into the world?

3. Each breath and each moment contains the lesson of resurrection, new life, letting go, death and rest. How have you experienced this cycle in your life and what have you learned by noticing it? Explore what you have needed to let go of in the past to be in the place you are at today. How has your trust in God's will deepened as a result? Has it made the inevitable return to the cycle easier to accept and embrace?

4. How does the song of the milkweed help you heal and grow?

5. Christ's friends did not stay awake in the garden while Christ was reckoning with God's will. Explore who is awake or trying to be awake for you in your life. Explore whether you are being asked to be awake for another.

6. What is stirring in you as a response to the moment? Do you have a creative call or something stronger to write a poem, paint a picture, do a dance, or sing a new song? Do you feel a nudge to take a walk, sit in silence, talk to a friend,

or start some new venture? Try it. What encouragement do you need? Ask for it. How might you share it in faith to heal someone else?

7. What other Scriptural passages sing The Milkweed song? Look here to start: Luke 22:39–45, Luke 15:11–25.

CONCLUSION

Ah, here we are at the conclusion. Are we done? Is this beautiful work, this healing way, and this disciplined engagement in the moment ever done? I hope not. What have we learned? What have we found? Do you sense, as I do, that we must return again, and again, and again to listen, explore, learn, and grow? Do you awe, as I do, that God's teachings for us in each moment are ever-deeper, ever-more healing, and eternally available? The birch tree taught us of waiting and growth. We will, undoubtedly, need that lesson again and will return in a new, maybe deeper, place to sing with the birch. We learned of hunger and abundance from the fragments and of mercy and surprise from the Good Samaritan. Yes, we will return again. From the narrows, we became what—resigned, enamored, comforted—by the circling in and out of life, persevering over and over again? We were shown that there is mystery and unknowing in every moment, and that we must, ultimately, journey with the milkweed to the let go and accept again, and again, and again.

I am wondering about this return, over and over, to God, and wondering, too, if it is in the process of return that a life of beauty is made. Life circles us in and out and around, again and again. Seasons come around, again and again. When they do, I am often surprisingly caught off-guard to find myself back to mulling over the past or trying to control the future in a new situation. I'm back to looking for the living among the dead, for healing among those that are not able to offer it, and to the world for something that can only come from God. And so we return—we start again. We retreat to this present moment and ask God for help, again. Help is there. We pray, take a walk, sit still, sing, and write again, and somehow, in this return, we grow into ourselves, grow into God's depths in us, and make something beautiful with it all. Healing happens. Have you ever noticed that famous artists go through certain periods of work? They paint the same image in new ways over and over again. Not long ago, I saw an exhibit of countless sketches of bullfights by Picasso. It seems Picasso returned again and again and again to sketch the bloody bullfight—from a new angle, with a different pencil, comingled with new characters and colors—and, somehow, when considered all together, a breathtaking masterpiece of works was made.

Whether you have made a decision to retreat for a week or just a hour; whether you have been guided to change something big or small in your relationship with God, yourself, or someone else; whether you reckon with the small and large deaths in your life with pen in hand, in the woods, in the stillness of meditation, in dancing, photography, singing, conversation . . . however you return, my prayer is that you will receive the fruits and healing of this moment, that you will experience the rest and the resurrection, again, and again, and again, that you will see the beautiful masterpiece and hear the rich song of it all. I offer you, here in the end, what I offered in the beginning—a poem—a way that I reckon with it all again, and again, and again.

Again and Again and Again.
Here, again and again.
Searching this place of hardware and steel
for bread.
Again and Again and Again.
Here, again and again.
Searching this race for the living among
the dead.
Again and Again and Again.

Picasso again paints the bull
the goring, the blood, and the kiss.
The mad pull the trigger.
The crazed point the finger.
The artist with brush, song, or pen,
again and again and again,
paint to remember
sing crazy to find
write madly and angry to win.
Again and Again and Again.

Picasso again paints the bull
the goring, the blood, and the kiss.
The judges to churches.
The lusting to schools.
The lonely to love songs
and dreams filled with fools.
Chasing forsaken
begging disgrace
shackled to trigger
the whole human race
and shackled to paintbrush and pen.
Again and Again and Again.

Again, somehow, in again
in again, the painting is made.
The blood, bull, and kiss,
the bread, death, and steel,
again, land on the same page.
This life of the crazed
makes beauty and song.
The forsaken belong.
The prodigal son, again, loved all along.
Again and Again and Again.

Again and Again and Again.
Here I am singing again.
Singing again of doors slamming closed
on arms that are offering bread.
Singing of blood from knives drawn for death
stopped by the healer with knives carving breath.
The assassin and surgeon
the bull and the kiss
a prayer that makes living
the dead.
Again and Again and Again.

BIBLIOGRAPHY

The World Community of Christian Meditation, "What is Meditation." Online: http://www.wccm.org/content/what-meditation

The World Community of Christian Meditation, "The Mantra." Online: http://www.wccm.org/content/what-meditation